B.E. S.E.E.N.

FOR USE WITH THE NOVEL, THE PRICE WE PAY
BY NIKKI T. ANTHONY

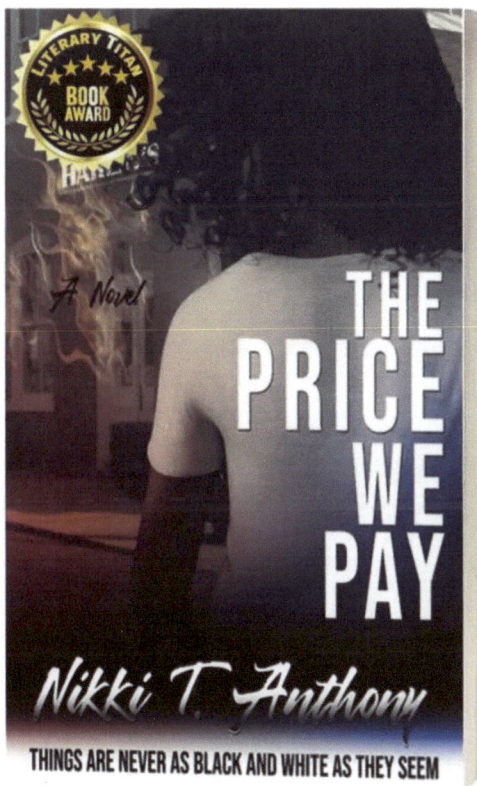

A Novel

THE PRICE WE PAY

LITERARY TITAN
BOOK AWARD

Nikki T. Anthony

THINGS ARE NEVER AS BLACK AND WHITE AS THEY SEEM

Study Guide

B.I.A.S. Education & Techniques
for Overcoming Bias with Practical
Examples and Illustrations

Guide Created by Brandy M. Miller
Edited by Joylynn M. Ross

B.E. S.E.E.N.: Bias Education & Techniques / Brandy M. Miller
1. Non-Fiction-Interpersonal Relationships
2. Non-Fiction-Bias; Prejudices; Racism
3. Non-Fiction-Study Guide
4. Non-Fiction-Resource
5. Non-Fiction-Communication Skills

eBook ISBN-13: 978-1-63627-007-4
Print ISBN;13: 978-1-63627-008-1

Cataloging-in-Publication Data is on file with the Library of Congress

Print edition printed in the United States of America

10 9 8 7 6 5 4 3 2 1

First Edition

CONTENTS

Introduction

Hello!

While The Price We Pay is fiction, the experiences outlined in its pages are pulled from real life. Every person in these pages is impacted, in one way or another, by their own B.I.A.S. and the B.I.A.S. of those around them.

It's our hope that as you work through this study guide you can begin to recognize the impact of B.I.A.S. wherever it appears in your life so you can Take the L.E.A.D. in deciding how you want to handle it rather than reacting and responding to what others say and do.

Nikki T. Anthony

Using *The Price We Pay*

We're going to use chapter 1 of The Price We Pay, a novel by Nikki T. Anthony, as the foundation for this guide to help us better understand bias, how it impacts our interpersonal relationships and communities, and then to formulate plans to counteract bias where necessary.

While the story itself is fictional, the events are based on the author's real-life experiences and perceptions as seen through her eyes. Naturally, there will be biases involved in the way the story is told, as bias is an unavoidable part of the human experience.

The first challenge we have is to identify those biases and determine whether they are helpful or harmful.

The second challenge, once we've identified the harmful biases, is to create concrete plans of action that allow us to overcome them.

Suggested prerequisites before using this study guide and for it to be most effective and have the greatest impact in understanding, challenging, and overcoming both your own biases and those of others:

1. Read chapter 1, at minimum, of the award-winning novel, The Price We Pay by Nikki T. Anthony. If you have not yet purchased your copy, you can do so directly from the publisher at https://ptppress.com/books
2. Take the B.E. S.E.E.N. Course by visiting https://ptppress.com/courses
3. Complete the B.E. S.E.E.N. workbook included with the companion course.

Now, let's begin!

Chapter 1

B.I.A.S. in Action

Our story begins with Zenetta Henchman being sent to Harlin's, a neighborhood store, to purchase some Alaga cane syrup for a meal that Herschel Henchman, her father, is preparing for the family.

Zenetta's biases begin making themselves evident starting in the next few lines. She carries deep biases against her father:

- His pride and ego cost him everything
- He's got a lack of empathy
- He's proud of being the only one of his kind on the Buzzardville Police Force
- He contributes to the destruction of Buzzardville
- He's part of the problem
- He lacks the ability to understand others
- He makes excuses for the people that run Harlin's

B.I.A.S. can be summarized as the set of beliefs, ideas, assumptions, and stories that we tell ourselves about each other and about the motivations behind behaviors that we see.

She also carries biases against Harlin's, the closest grocery store:

- It's small
- It's rundown
- It smells like dead meat
- Everything's overpriced
- Everything's poorly managed
- The Koreans that run the store overcharges the folks in the neighborhood
- They don't deliver what they charge the neighborhood for
- They make it clear that they don't like Black people
- They watch the Black people like a hawk whenever they enter the store
- They set up shop in their area because Black neighborhoods are dirt cheap compared to other areas

B.I.A.S. in Action (Cont.)

BIAS Reinforcing Behaviors

Zenetta's biases against the Korean store clerk are reinforced by the way the clerk acts toward Ju-Ju when Zenetta arrives at Harlin's. She tells us that the clerk:

- **Eyeballs Ju-Ju as she and her friend argue**
- **Shouts, "Hurry up and make a decision or get your thieving behinds out!"**

Obviously, the store clerk carries her own biases toward Ju-Ju and her friend.

Ju-Ju Responds to the Clerk's B.I.A.S.

Zenetta tells us that Ju-Ju responds to this accusation in anger:

- **Her face contorted, her cheeks flushed, her eyes sparkled with ferocity**
- **Ju-Ju stares at the clerk, unblinking, as if her eyes "were being used as a weapon"**

A Clash of Cultures

Zenetta admits that the look Ju-Ju gives the store clerk "frightened the life out of me, to the point where I couldn't move."

She states, "a look of terror overtook" the clerk's face as she pleads, "I don't want any trouble. Make a decision and leave my store."

Ju-Ju follows up the stare with a clear threat to the clerk, "You think you can come into our neighborhood and treat us like we animals? You'll be lucky if I don't bust your head to the white meat before I leave this store."

Then, Ju-Ju reaches into her pocket. Zenetta tells us it's to hand the clerk a ten-dollar bill. However, the clerk reaches for a shotgun and fires two shots into Ju-Ju's forehead.

A fifteen-year-old girl lies dead. All because of bias.

The Continuing Impact of BIAS

Impacting Interpretation of Events

Zenetta runs home from the crime scene and displays more bias, telling her father on the way in the door, "She shot her! She shot her for no reason!"

This demonstrates Zenetta's belief that a threat, such as the one Ju-Ju made to the clerk, is no reason to shoot even though Zenetta herself admits to being frightened by it.

However, from the clerk's point of view, that threat was directed at her.

Is it possible she was even more frightened than Zenetta? To the point that she took the threat seriously enough to react based on that fear...whether it was a right or wrong action to take?

Affecting Her Attitude Toward Police

A police sergeant she doesn't know shows up to force Zenetta to go down to the station to tell her version of what happened at Harlin's. She admits the interview "turned out to be not as bad as I thought it would be."

This statement shows us that Zenetta had a bias before going to the station. She assumed the police wouldn't treat her well, which is why she's surprised it wasn't as bad as she thought it would be. That attitude might have colored the responses she did get from the police.

Zenetta wants the police to "Grab the handcuffs, open the jail cell, close the jail cell, and throw away the key. End of story," as far as the store clerk is concerned. That's the only way she'll feel that justice was done.

The Continuing Impact of BIAS

Making Assumptions (the "A" in Bias

Zenetta knows the store clerk isn't going to be arrested, but assumes it's . . .

> ". . . because unlike people who looked like me, the Korean store clerk had the complexion for the protection. In fact, I wouldn't have been surprised if the clerk didn't serve one day of jail time for what she did to Ju-Ju."

Zenetta's bias is based on past experiences, as we'll learn in future chapters. She's seen people of light complexions get away with injustices while she, and other people who are darker skinned, aren't afforded that same privilege.

She also makes a lot of assumptions about the officer taking her statement, telling us he:

- Hardly looked interested in what I had to say
- Lifted his thick eyebrows high above his beady eyes every time I answered a question
- Seemed to question the validity of every word I spoke
- Was forced to listen to her because it was his job
- Didn't care that this experience was traumatic for her

All of these biases color how Zenetta sees and feels about the events. They also color her reactions and behaviors, affecting the way that people treat her without her even being aware of it.

> Every character in this chapter is responding and reacting to their own internal biases, with disastrous impact for the lives of the people involved.

Your Work To Do

Read and Answer the Following Questions

1. Did you have your own biases about this chapter (the characters, situations, environments, actions, etc.) prior to reading chapter 1 of this study guide? If so, list them.

_____

_____

_____

_____

_____

_____

_____

_____

_____

_____

_____

_____

_____

_____

_____

Your Work To Do

Read and Answer the Following Questions

2. Have any of your biases changed or been challenged? If so, which ones and how do you see things now versus how you saw them before you went through this exercise?

_____

_____

_____

_____

_____

_____

_____

_____

_____

_____

_____

_____

_____

_____

Your Work To Do

3. After reading chapter 1 of this study guide, do you understand more about the biases displayed by the characters in chapter 1 of The Price We Pay? Do you find them valid or invalid?

_____

_____

_____

_____

_____

_____

_____

_____

_____

_____

_____

_____

_____

_____

Chapter 2

Seeking to S.E.R.V.E. the Neighborhood

We've identified some key points where bias is coloring how people react and respond to one another within the neighborhood. If we want to help create a better and more peaceful Buzzardville, we need to adopt an attitude of service.

S.eeking the Best for All People

If we want to serve the neighborhood, that means we need to look for the best possible outcome for everyone involved—the store clerk included. We need to be willing to look for solutions that allow everyone to win.

E.ducating Ourselves About Their Desires, Goals, and Frustrations

Our next step in service is to seek to educate ourselves about what each person desires and their goals along with what's currently frustrating them or presenting them with an obstacle.

Only once we get a firm view on what each person wants - and what they believe is stopping them from getting there - are we prepared to search for a win-win solution that works for each person.

R.especting Everyone's Opinions

An attitude of respect for people's opinions and contributions helps put the people around us at ease. We don't have to agree with how they see things, say things, or do things, but we need to respect those things or they're unlikely to share it with us.

Seeking to S.E.R.V.E. the Neighborhood (Cont.)

V.aluing Them and Their Contributions

People who feel valued are more likely to make contributions. People whose contributions are valued—even when they are small or inadequate to solving the whole problem—are more likely to continue making contributions. If we're going to help solve the neighborhood's problems, we're going to need as many people making their contributions as possible.

E.ngaging Your Problem-Solving Skills

Now that you know what's needed and wanted in the neighborhood, we're ready to engage those problem-solving skills and come up with unique solutions that ensure everyone wins.

Your Work To Do

Read and Answer the Following Questions

1. Do you find it difficult to see and seek the best in each character in chapter 1 of The Price We Pay?

_____

_____

2. If so, which character(s) is/are toughest for you to relate to?

_____

_____

_____

_____

_____

3. Which of your own biases, if any, are making it tough for you?

_____

_____

_____

_____

_____

_____

Your Work To Do

4. If you're easily able to see and seek the best in everyone, what strategies do you use to help you keep that positive mindset?

_____

_____

_____

_____

_____

5. Do you see anyone who doesn't feel valued in this chapter?

_____

_____

_____

6. What could you do to help change that?

_____

_____

_____

_____

Chapter 3

Empathizing By Asking the Right Questions

Questions Help Us Challenge Our Beliefs and Assumptions

Challenging our beliefs and assumptions about why people do what they do begins with asking ourselves the right questions to be able to put ourselves in their shoes.
We need to take a step back from the emotion of the events and look at things through an objective lens.

That's hard to do in the heat of the moment, as our emotions tend to take over.

Emotions live in our subconscious and make decisions for us at 27,000 times the speed of our logical, reasoning processing center of the brain.

That's why developing the ability to check our emotions is an important skill to develop.

Re-Examining Ju-Ju's Shooting

We learn that the clerk carries a shotgun behind the counter.

1. Why does the clerk carry a gun behind the counter?

People who are confident of their safety and security don't generally keep guns at hand.

2. Why does the clerk assume the teenagers arguing with one another are there to steal?

People who haven't experienced people trying to steal from them don't automatically assume that someone is going to steal from them.

Empathizing By Asking the Right Questions (Cont.)

Additional Questions

These two points can lead us to some additional questions:

3. Are there people in the neighborhood stealing from the store?
4. If so, is it going unaddressed by the parents, neighborhood residents, or police?

We can also examine Ju-Ju's behavior:

5. Why did Ju-Ju feel it was okay to threaten the clerk?
6. Did Ju-Ju know her behavior was dangerous?

The right questions can lead to a re-evaluation of the events from a new perspective and help shed light on the "why" behind "what" happened.

This leads to still another question:

7. Did the clerk take Ju-Ju's threat seriously?

Re-Examining Ju-Ju's Shooting

Zenetta admits that Ju-Ju's behavior frightened her, and she noticed the terror that the clerk felt, so this begs another question:

8. Why did Zenetta not see the clerk's reaction to Ju-Ju's threat to "bust your head to the white meat before I leave this store" as a possible response to what reads as a threat to the woman's life? Not to say the response was the right response to take.

Empathizing By Asking the Right Questions (Cont.)

Diving into Matters

After examining all of these questions, we're prepared to dive into the matter at hand.

9. Is this a matter of culture?
10. Is it normal for the people in Ju-Ju and Zenetta's neighborhood to threaten one another with violence they don't intend to carry out?
11. Is this culture of threatening unintended violence the reason Zenetta sees Ju-Ju's threats as no big deal?
12. If so, does the clerk know that?

A Change in Perspective

What isn't told to us is anything about the clerk's background history. We don't know if she's carrying the gun in her store because someone she cares about died when someone tried to rob them. What we do know is that she felt terrified and responded accordingly.

13. Seen in this light, is it possible the reason she didn't face jail time was because the police saw her act of shooting Ju-Ju as an act of self-defense, rather than it being a case of racial privilege?

Asking the right questions before drawing conclusions is a great way to fight our own internal biases. It helps us to use our empathy, put ourselves in the shoes of the other parties, and get to the heart of what needs to change so that everyone can thrive and grow.

Your Work To Do

Honestly and thoroughly answer the questions asked in this chapter of the study guide.

1. Why do you think the clerk carries a gun behind the counter?

_____

_____

_____

_____

2. Why do you think the clerk assumes the teenagers arguing with one another are there to steal?

_____

_____

_____

_____

3. Do you think there are people in the neighborhood stealing?

_____

_____

_____

_____

Your Work To Do

Honestly and thoroughly answer the questions asked in this chapter of the study guide.

4. If you think there are people stealing, do you think it's being addressed by parents, the neighborhood, or police?

_____

_____

_____

_____

5. Why do you think Ju-Ju felt it was okay to threaten the clerk?

_____

_____

_____

_____

6. Do you think Ju-Ju knew her behavior was dangerous?

_____

_____

_____

_____

Your Work To Do

7. Do you think the clerk took Ju-Ju's threats seriously?

_____

_____

_____

_____

8. Why do you think Zenetta did not see the clerk's reaction to Ju-Ju's threat to "bust your head to the white meat before I leave this store" as a possible response to what reads as a threat to the woman's life?

_____

_____

_____

_____

9. Do you think this is a matter of culture?

_____

_____

_____

_____

Your Work To Do

Honestly and thoroughly answer the questions asked in this chapter of the study guide.

10. Do you think it is normal for the people in Ju-Ju and Zenetta's neighborhood to threaten one another with violence they don't intend to carry out? What evidence do you see of that?

_____

_____

_____

_____

11. Do you think this possible culture of threatening unintended violence is the reason Zenetta sees Ju-Ju's threats as no big deal?

_____

_____

_____

_____

12. If so, do you think the clerk knows that?

_____

_____

_____

_____

Your Work To Do

Honestly and thoroughly answer the questions asked in this chapter of the study guide.

13. Do you think it's possible the police saw the clerk's shooting of Ju-Ju as an act of self-defense? Why or why not?

_____

_____

_____

_____

14. Evaluate and re-examine your answers. Are any personal biases or experiences influencing them? If so, what are some of those personal biases or experiences?

_____

_____

_____

_____

_____

_____

Chapter 4

Empowerment: Equipping Everyone to Benefit

CREATING THE CONDITIONS FOR COMMUNITIES TO THRIVE

Communities can't thrive and grow when only some people can B.E. S.E.E.N.!

Let's look at how we can ensure that everyone benefits from participating in the conversation.

REMEMBER: EMPOWERMENT IS NOT ENABLING

Despite popular belief and the opinion of some when teaching and training on the topic of bias, everyone has power and privilege. It's a matter of identifying it in certain situations, circumstances, and environments. In fact, empowering means showing someone who is already powerful where their power lies and when and how to use it. We are all powerful, and telling someone otherwise could be inadvertently enabling them.

Empowerment: Equipping Everyone to Benefit (Cont.)

ENABLING VERSUS EMPOWERING

Enabling people means we take care of the problem for them because they aren't capable of handling things on their own.

Empowering people puts the right tools in people's hands to take care of the problem for themselves.

WE MUST BELIEVE THAT THEY CAN

We must believe that the store clerk, Ju-Ju, and Zenetta are capable of being reasonable and working together toward a common goal if given the right tools for the job.

They may not get it right during this first conversation or the first hundred or even first thousand times they try, but if they don't quit and keep trying, there will be a breakthrough.

THERE'S VALUE IN THE EFFORT ITSELF

A lot of their learning and growth will come from tackling these challenges and pushing through the inevitable frustrations that arise.

Empowering Zenetta, Ju-Ju, and the Store Clerk (Cont.)

FACILITATING THE CONVERSATION

We are there to facilitate the conversation, not hold it for them. We want to equip them with the tools, skills, and education needed for future success without us.

THEY WILL NEED OUR ENCOURAGEMENT

Ju-Ju, Zentta, and the store clerk are going to be tempted to give up on the efforts to engage in productive conversations with every failure. We need to be there to support them, cheer them on, and remind them that failure is part of learning.

IT REQUIRES PATIENCE AND PERSISTENCE

These skills aren't easy to learn or to master. They're going to slip into old habits and ways of thinking. We just need to remind them of what's at stake if they don't persist and then support them in being patient with themselves, each other, and the process.

Empowering Zenetta, Ju-Ju, and the Store Clerk (Cont.)

LISTENING TO COMPLAINTS

We can learn a lot about what people want by listening to what they complain about. What are they getting that they don't want or not getting that they do want?

ZENETTA'S COMPLAINTS ABOUT HARLIN'S

- It's small
- It's rundown
- It smells like dead meat
- Everything's overpriced
- Everything's poorly managed
- The Korean owners overcharge the folks in the neighborhood
- They don't deliver what they charge the neighborhood for
- They make it clear they don't like Black people
- They watch Black people like a hawk whenever they enter the store
- They set up shop in their area because Black neighborhoods are dirt cheap compared to other areas

WHAT ZENETTA WANTS

- A larger space
- A well-stocked store in good repair
- Meat and produce that are fresh
- Reasonable prices
- Efficient store management
- To feel welcomed by the clerk
- To be treated with an assumption of good intention, rather than suspicion

JU-JU'S COMPLAINTS

- Being called a thief
- Being treated like animals

Empowering Zenetta, Ju-Ju, and the Store Clerk (Cont.)

WHAT JU-JU WANTS

- Not to be falsely accused of something she's not done
- To be treated with an assumption of good intention, rather than with suspicion
- To be respected as a person

THE STORE CLERK'S COMPLAINTS

- Get your thieving behinds out
- I don't want any trouble

WHAT THE STORE CLERK WANTS

- For people not to steal from her
- A trouble-free environment

KNOWING WHAT EVERYONE WANTS IS WHERE NEGOTIATION BEGINS!

WHAT WE CAN ALSO GUESS THE STORE CLERK WANTS:

Based on the fact she runs a business (or her employer does) we can guess she wants:

- To make a maximum profit at minimum expense
- To attract more customers to her store

Only once it's clear what everyone wants are you ready to begin negotiations. If you aren't sure you know all that each party desires, keep asking, "And what else?" until there's nothing else they can think of. This will make negotiations much easier.

Your Work To Do:

1. What are some solutions you can think of to help everyone get what they want?

_____

_____

_____

_____

_____

_____

_____

_____

_____

_____

_____

_____

_____

_____

_____

Your Work To Do (Cont.)

_____

_____

_____

_____

_____

_____

_____

_____

_____

_____

_____

_____

_____

_____

Chapter 5

Negotiation: Ensuring Everyone Wins

LOOKING FOR COMMON GROUND

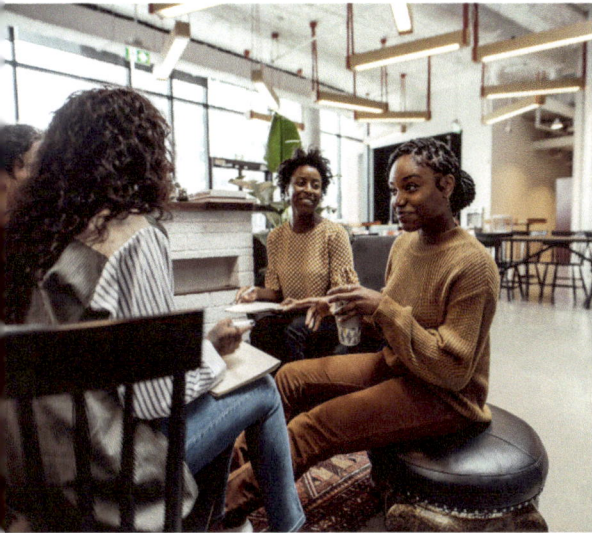

We need to look for some common ground between Zenetta, Ju-Ju, and the store clerk. So, we'll start by looking at what everyone seems to want.

We can assume neither Zenetta nor Ju-Ju want trouble. That's not why they came. All three people share in common wanting a trouble-free environment.

The store clerk, like Zenetta and Ju-Ju, wants to be treated with an assumption of good intention, rather than with suspicion.

So, those two points are where we'll begin our conversation, because it's the easiest place to gain agreement.

WHERE DO THEIR INTERESTS CONFLICT?

Zenetta's interests in lower prices, fresh meat and produce, a larger space, and a well-stocked store in good repair might conflict with the store clerk's interest in maximizing her profit for minimum expense. They'll need to negotiate to find a way past that potential conflict.

Negotiation: Ensuring Everyone Wins (Cont.)

JU-JU AND THE STORE CLERK: WHAT HAPPENS WHEN WE DON'T SUCCEED

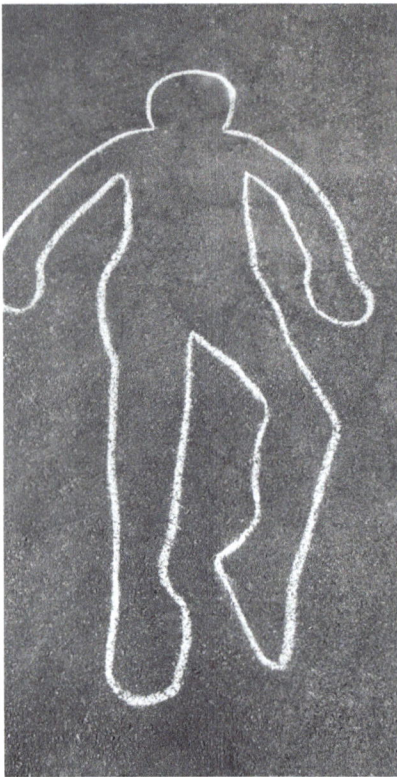

Ju-Ju and the store clerk both lost because neither could overcome their biases. Ju-Ju not only didn't get the product she wanted to purchase, she didn't get the respect she desired, either.

The store clerk not only didn't get the money she could have made from Ju-Ju's purchase, she got more trouble than she could imagine with her choice in how to handle the interaction with Ju-Ju.

HELPING ZENETTA STRATEGIZE WAYS OF WINNING

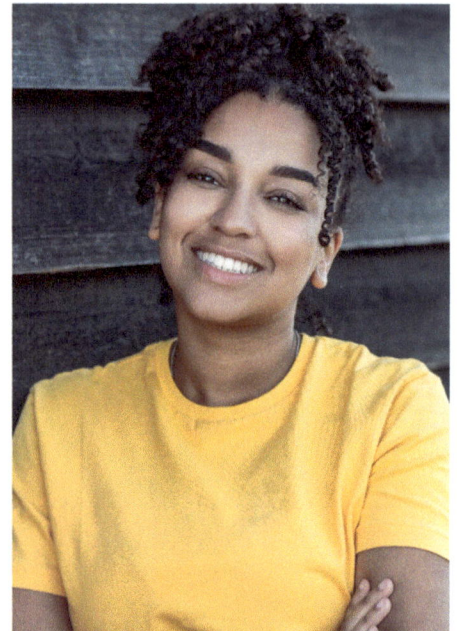

For Zenetta to win, she needs to put together a plan that allows the store clerk to get what she wants by giving Zenetta what she wants. That may seem impossible, but it's not.

We can assume that if Ju-Ju and Zenetta and Momma all feel unwelcome in Harlin's, they're not alone. That means Harlins is probably losing out on potential profits they could make if they listened to their customer base and found ways to deliver.

Negotiation: Ensuring Everyone Wins(Cont.)

If Zenetta, Momma, or other members of the community can show Harlin's how to do that without the massive outlays of cash they might not have, they will not only be getting what they want, they'll be helping the store achieve their goals of increasing profits and attracting more customers.

COMPLAINTS ARE FINE. SOLUTIONS ARE BETTER.

It's perfectly fine to bring to someone's attention an issue or a problem you see, but it's always better if you can bring a potential solution when you do. People can brush off criticism after a while, even when it's valid, because they may not have the knowledge or resources needed to deal with it.

If you come with a solution, that can be a game changer. It shows you're truly interested in helping improve things and aren't merely expecting other people to do it for you.

FINDING CREATIVE SOLUTIONS

Making a store feel larger can be a matter of how products are placed in the aisles, how much lighting is shown in areas, and even where mirrors are placed. It's possible that a little interior design work could solve the problem of making Harlin's feel like it's got more space than it actually does. Helping the clerk to solve that problem could even help the clerk win more customers, ensuring she's making more profits with less expense.

Negotiation: Ensuring Everyone Wins (Cont.)

A PROBABLE REASON FOR THE PROBLEM

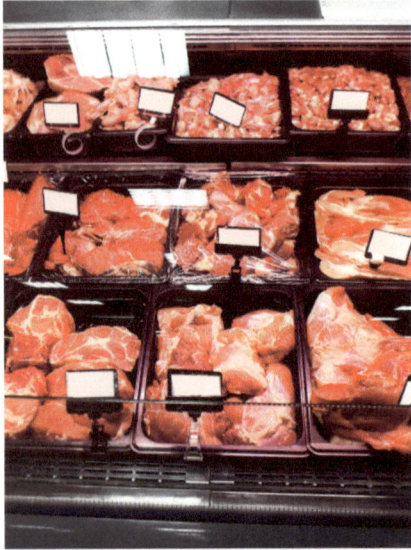

A probable reason for the meat and produce already going bad by the time the store clerk stocks it is that the owners are buying the meat and produce that didn't sell from one Stop at a deep discount, and then marking it up for their store. If Zenetta, Momma, or the community of Buzzardville can do a little research and find out how much Harlin's is spending at One Stop and then give them an alternative that is at the same price or less with a higher quality product, that will solve problems for the entire neighborhood.

EMPOWERING YOURSELF FOR NEGOTIATION

It might seem like this is doing the work that the clerk or store owners should be doing themselves, but in reality, this is a low-key way of letting the clerk or store owners know that:

1. You know what's going on and aren't willing to allow yourself to be taken advantage of;
2. You understand their need to make a profit and you find value enough in their presence in the neighborhood that you're willing to work with them on that while at the same time wanting better for yourself
3. You're capable of offering a better alternative to the neighborhood if they aren't willing to help you, but you'd rather give them a chance to do the right thing first

> Your time spent educating yourself on how things work will empower you to enter negotiations on an equal footing.

Negotiation: Ensuring Everyone Wins (Cont.)

CREATING ADDITIONAL OPTIONS

Of course, it's possible the store clerk or the owners won't be willing to negotiate with Zenetta. They may think they don't need to or that Zenetta can't help them.

However, that doesn't mean that's the end of things. Momma points out that they shouldn't have to travel across town to get what should be available right in their own neighborhood. She's right, but Harlin's isn't their only option.

INVESTING IN THE FUTURE THEY DESIRE

We learned in Chapter 1 that Momma owns Buzzards Row. She rents out the homes to the people on the street. Zenetta mentioned that real estate in their part of town was dirt cheap compared to suburban areas like Woodland Hills. Could Momma take some of her profits and invest them in purchasing a plot of land to create a community garden?

Could the neighborhood pool their money to build their own grocery store and stock it? Could Zenetta spearhead the charge to do those things?

Empowering Zenetta means helping her think through alternative options and then equipping her with the tools to pursue whatever route she's chosen.

Having these additional options - including the option to be able to walk away from Harlin's altogether - is a critical point to the next phase of negotiation.

Negotiation: Ensuring Everyone Wins (Cont.)

FOSTER A SPIRIT OF COOPERATION

The alternatives to Harlin's are going to require hefty investments of time, effort, money, and resources. It's in everyone's best interests if the negotiations can succeed.

We want to encourage the store clerk's participation in the process so that it feels like a cooperative venture, rather than a competition where only one party can win.

Zenetta might want to consider that Harlin's is a business, and it is meant to turn a profit. That profit doesn't have to be at the neighborhood's expense, though. It's reasonable for the neighborhood to insist the business live up to certain standards.

Everyone's concerns and considerations should be taken into account before the conversation begins.

WHAT CAN BE COMPROMISED? WHAT CAN'T BE?

Since we can't ask, we can assume that the store clerk can't compromise on the need to make a profit. That's why Harlin's exists, and it's only reasonable to expect that it profits or it will end up closing its doors.

Negotiation: Ensuring Everyone Wins (Cont.)

EXPECTING FAIR TREATMENT

Another thing that can't be compromised, for Zenetta, is the way the store clerk treats the members of the neighborhood. She needs to find out the underlying cause behind the store clerk's unwelcoming and unfriendly behavior.

Is it prejudice? Or is it maybe a case of poor mental health? Does the store clerk - just as Ju-Ju and Zenetta don't feel welcomed in the store - maybe not feel welcomed in the neighborhood?

If it's a case of miscommunication, this is Zenetta's chance to apologize for any contributions made by her behavior (being the first is the first step in taking the LEAD!) and then clarifying why she's acted the way she has. Perhaps the store clerk will do the same in return.

WHAT TAKING THE L.E.A.D. IN THE CONVERSATION LOOKS LIKE FOR ZENETTA

L.isten to understand the store clerk's point of view

E.mpathize with her position and try to put yourself in her shoes

A.sk her relevant questions to be sure you understand the situation fully

D.evelop win-win situations where you both get what you want

Keep going until both parties reach an agreement about the outcome. The Goal: Everyone walks away feeling like a winner!

Your Work To Do

1. Pretend that you are the store clerk. Take the L.E.A.D. in a conversation with Ju-Ju. Write what that conversation might look like.

_____

_____

_____

_____

_____

_____

_____

_____

_____

_____

_____

_____

_____

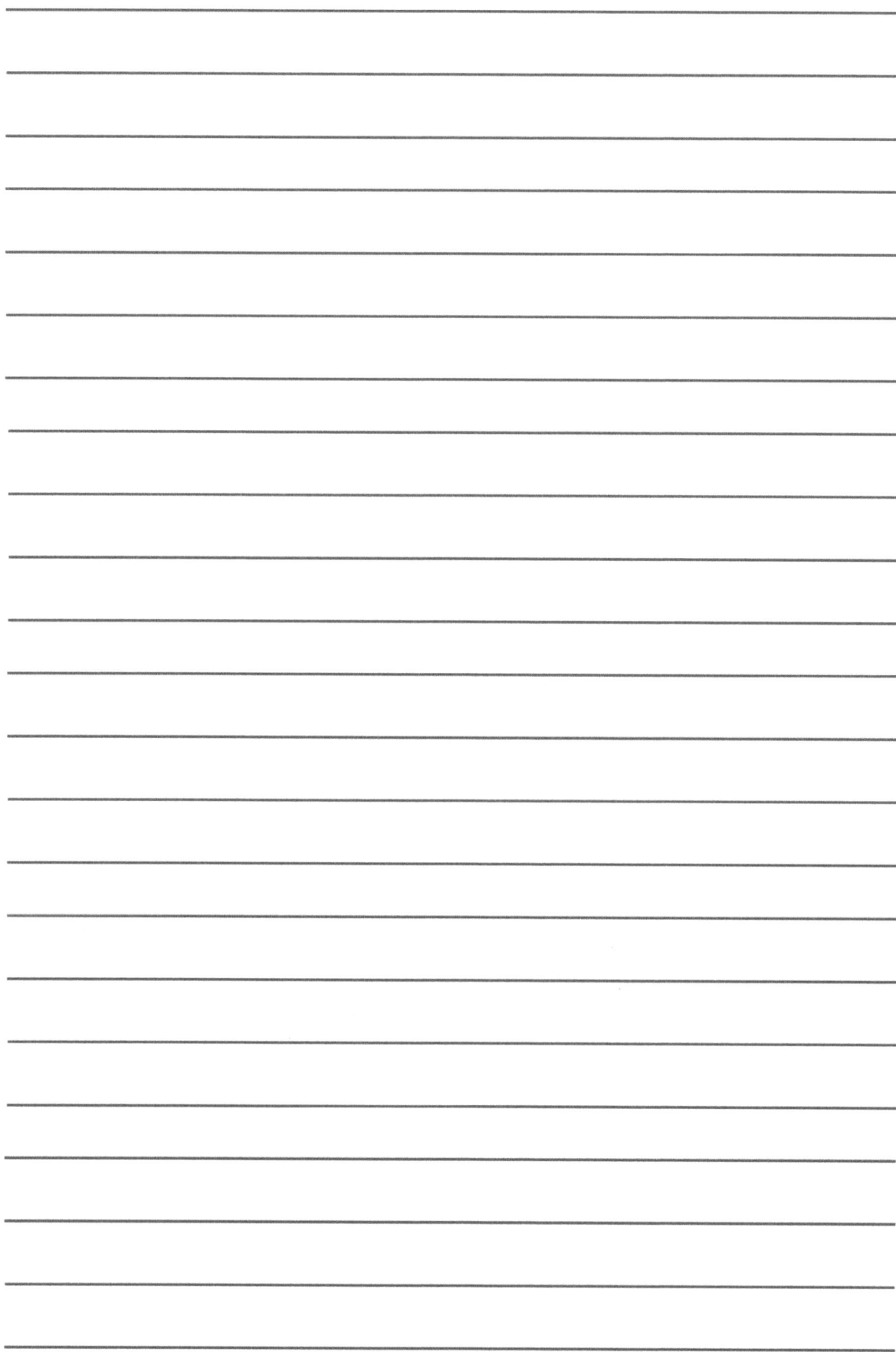

Your Work To Do

1. Pretend that you are Ju-Ju. Take the L.E.A.D. in a conversation with the store clerk. Write what the conversation might look like.

_____

_____

_____

_____

_____

_____

_____

_____

_____

_____

_____

_____

_____

_____

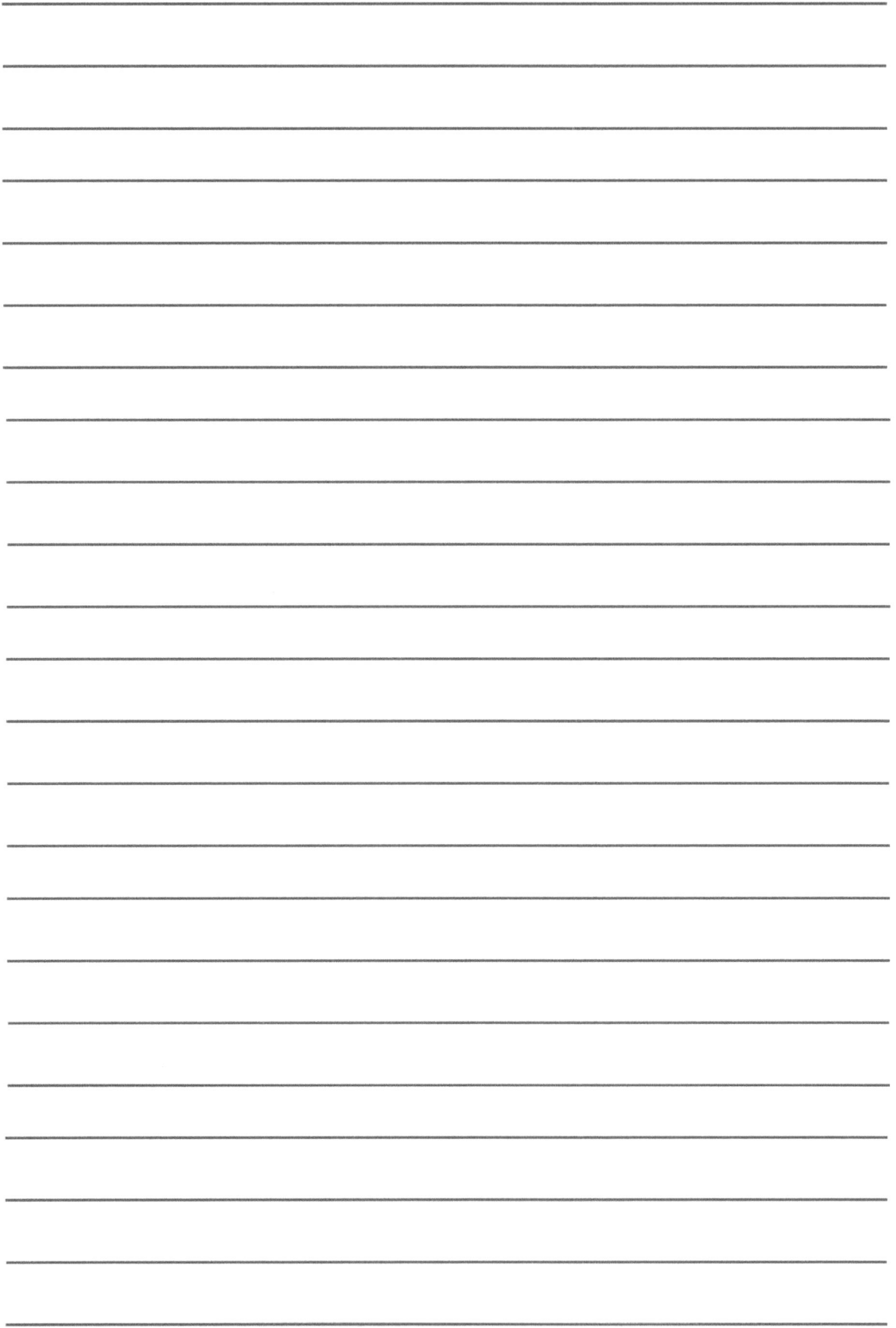

Conclusion

CONGRATULATIONS!!

You've reached the end of the B.E. S.E.E.N. study guide. Now, it's time to do your best to apply this new information, skills, and techniques to your everyday life.

If you have not yet taken the B.E. S.E.E.N. course, now is the time to do that. Bring this guide with you. If you have taken the course, use this guide to practice engaging in conversations as you read through the pages.

What's Next?

1. Visit https://pathtoconnections.com/courses
2. Sign up for our R.I.S.E. U.P. and L.E.A.D. course so you can learn how to engage in difficult and uncomfortable conversations, as well as controversial topics, in any mix of company you might find yourself in, no matter how challenging the environment.
3. Sign up for our Take the L.E.A.D. training where we go into more detail about how to L.E.A.D. challenging conversations
4. Take our 5 Steps to Get Anyone to Lean In and Listen to You FREE course